Stylish
weddings

An Imprint of Sterling Publishing
387 Park Avenue South
New York, NY 10016

ISBN 978-1-4547-0412-6

Doh, Jenny.
  Stylish weddings : 50 simple ideas to make from top designers / Jenny Doh.
-- First edition.
    pages cm
  ISBN 978-1-4547-0412-6
  1. Handicraft. 2. Wedding decorations. I. Title.
  TT149.D64 2014
  745.594'1--dc23
                              2012046619

Distributed in Canada by Sterling Publishing
c/o Canadian Manda Group, 165 Dufferin Street
Toronto, Ontario, Canada M6K 3H6
Distributed in the United Kingdom by GMC Distribution Services
Castle Place, 166 High Street, Lewes, East Sussex, England BN7 1XU
Distributed in Australia by Capricorn Link (Australia) Pty. Ltd.
P.O. Box 704, Windsor, NSW 2756, Australia

For information about custom editions, special sales, and premium and corporate purchases, please contact
Sterling Special Sales at 800-805-5489 or specialsales@sterlingpublishing.com.

Email academic@larkbooks.com for information about desk and examination copies.
The complete policy can be found at larkcrafts.com.

Manufactured in China

2 4 6 8 10 9 7 5 3 1

larkcrafts.com

Stylish weddings

50 Simple Ideas to Make from Top Designers

JENNY DOH

LARK

Contents

Introduction

by Jenny Doh

The days leading up to a person's wedding have become arguably *as* or even more exciting than the actual wedding day itself. This is increasingly true today as highly creative brides and grooms find imaginative ways to infuse creativity and handmade goodness into every aspect of nuptial festivities.

Ask a creative bride why she chooses to make things for her wedding rather than just buy everything, and you'll likely hear a multi-faceted answer. One main reason is that a handmade wedding is an affordable wedding. Though making enough jam to fill a jelly jar for each guest takes time, making favors rather than buying them is a great way to cut costs.

The other major reason why a bride chooses to make things for her wedding is because something handmade always elevates occasions. The specialness informs guests about the unique personality, character, and taste of the bride and groom. It inspires guests to converse more meaningfully with one another as they enjoy the festivities. And finally, it helps create memories for all to treasure for years to come.

Stylish Weddings honors the growing enthusiasm amongst brides and grooms to plan and execute weddings and receptions that are steeped in the traditions of sincerely handmade. In this book you'll learn from six top designers who offer their best ideas and instruction categorized in their signature design styles. The designers are, in order of appearance:

- **Serena Thompson: The Farm Chicks**
- **Minna Mercke Schmidt: Natural and Organic**
- **Tiffany Kirchner-Dixon: Vintage Glam**
- **Heather Bullard: Romantic and Pretty**
- **Corey Amaro: French-Inspired**
- **Tracy Schultz: Rustic and Elegant DIY**

On behalf of the entire *Stylish Weddings* team, I am honored that you have selected this book and the projects created by these amazing designers to help you infuse handmade touches into your festivities. Without a doubt, your efforts will lead to an event that will be unforgettable.

The Farm Chicks
wedding

with serena thompson
with concept collaboration and co-styling by Alisa Lewis

www.thefarmchicks.com

For the country girl at heart, The Farm Chicks wedding includes a ceremony under twinkle lights in a barn, a fancy breakfast held against a backdrop of pine trees and wide open sky, and cheerful daisies and Billy Balls for bouquets. Serena Thompson—The Farm Chick herself—envisioned and executed this event, managing to make this wedding day both special and carefree.

festive and fancy on the farm

This intimate wedding was held on a farm in the beautiful Northwest, where the tone was set by a stunning barn, acres of greenery as far as the eye could see, and a long wooden table in a meadow. For a comfortable and inviting setting, the wedding was held in the late morning—giving guests plenty of time to wander around the locale in the afternoon after a festive breakfast to celebrate the happy couple.

The congratulatory breakfast included a waffle bar, and mini pancakes stacked on individual plates with tiny pitchers of syrup; parfaits of homemade granola, fresh fruit, and yogurt served in mason jars; mini quiches; eggs benedict served in individual cast iron skillets; French toast stacks with berries and cream; miniature Bundt cakes; and a crepe cake and a frosted butter cake made from scratch.

Serena's Advice for Newlyweds

Don't keep a mental list of the things that bother you about your spouse; instead, keep a mental list of what you love about them. Focus on the life you love, and it will all fall into place.

Even though the food was the ultimate in comfort, Serena dressed up the brunch table with a vintage lace runner, the best china, and handmade cloth napkins. There's something about eating the fanciest of meals in the middle of a grassy field that brings a festive air to the seemingly everyday location.

a country celebration

The wedding party attire added to the cheery, country feel of the wedding. Bridesmaids dressed in checkered dresses and sandals, while the groomsmen wore gingham button-down shirts, handmade bow ties, and boutonnieres with flowers picked from the farm. After the ceremony in the barn, under a ceiling of twinkle lights, the wedding party enjoyed a foot-stompin' local country band—banjo included—that played on the back of a flat-bed farm truck.

To decorate for the event, Serena gathered tables, chairs, dishware, flowers, and décor from her home and the homes of close friends and family. With crates and pails as servingware for the food and gathered fresh flowers from the backyard for centerpieces and bouquets, this really was the epitome of a down-home event—one where all who attended took part, and one that celebrated classic, friendly life on the farm.

Serena's Ingredients for a Terrific Wedding

- Family and friends
- Good music and dancing
- Delicious food

Boutonnieres

Boutonnieres for the groomsmen are an easy way to add style and color with little or no cost. Simply clip wildflowers and greenery from your yard, wrap the lower portion of a grouping with twine, and trim the plants evenly at the bottom. Attach the boutonnieres using long stick pins.

Bow Ties

Handmade bow ties allow you to utilize the colors, patterns, and fabric that best suit your theme, and they add a bit of personal charm to an otherwise store-bought outfit. Plus, they're easy and fun to make. The striped fabric on these bow ties has a classic vintage feel, while the colors are bright and fresh.

what you'll need

Two contrasting fabrics per bow tie, cut to measure as follows:
- bow fabric (green):
  6 x 3½ inches (15.2 x 8.9 cm)
- tie fabric (yellow):
  10 x 2 inches (25.4 x 5.1 cm)

Iron

Scissors

5 mm-wide roll of fusible bonding web

Pin back and hot glue gun (or safety pin)

what you do

1 Iron all fabric pieces.
2 Press under the edges of the bow fabric ¼ inch (6 mm) on all sides. Secure the edges by cutting strips of fusible web and fusing them under the folds according to manufacturer's instructions.
3 Make a knot in the center of the tie fabric. With the bow fabric right side up, pinch its center and place the knot in that center. Wrap the tie edges around the back. ⓐ ⓑ ⓒ
4 Holding the tie fabric in place from the back, lay the bow on your work surface and hot glue the back of the knotted tie in place.
5 Cut off the remaining tie fabric. Hot glue a pin back behind the knot, or use a safety pin.

a

b

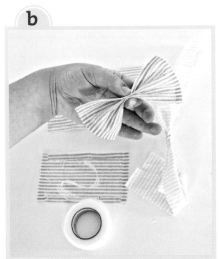

c

For the Entire Party

Make a tie for each groomsman. Consider using different fabrics for the best man if you want his tie to stand out from the others. Another idea is to make smaller bows and attach them to bobby pins, to be used as hair accessories by the bridesmaids.

Potato-Stamped napkins

Creating a handmade stamp out of a potato allows you the freedom to choose whatever shape you'd like, rather than relying on a premade stamp. Plus it's a subtle way to incorporate a handmade, farm chicks feel into another wedding item. When the event's over, save the stamped napkins—either as gifts for the bridal party or to keep in your own home.

what you'll need

Note: This yardage will yield four
　　20-inch (50.8 cm) square napkins

1¼ yards (1.2 m) of 44-inch
　　(111.8 cm) wide fabric

Iron

Pinking shears

Heart-shaped cookie cutter

Potato (with a diameter slightly larger
　　than the cookie cutter)

Kitchen knife

Cutting board

Fabric paint

Paper towel

Plate

Small cotton towel

what you do

1 Iron the fabric then cut it into
   20-inch (50.8 cm) squares using
   pinking shears. By using pinking
   shears, there is no need to hem
   the napkin edges.

2 Cut the potato in half using a
   cutting board and kitchen
   knife. ⓐ

3 Press the cookie cutter into the
   potato, and while the cutter is
   still in the potato, cut all around
   the cutter with the knife. ⓑ
   Remove the cut-off piece, and
   then remove the cookie cutter.
   ⓒ ⓓ

4 Squeeze a small amount of
   fabric paint onto a plate lined
   with a paper towel. Press the
   potato heart onto the paint and
   wipe any excess onto the paper
   towel. Press the heart onto the
   bottom center of each napkin.
   Let dry. ⓔ

5 Place a small cotton towel onto
   the stamped area and press with
   an iron to heat-set the paint.

Stamping on Fabric

Before pressing your stamp
onto the napkins, do a few test
stamps on a scrap of fabric to
determine the best technique
for you. Also, depending on the
weight of the fabric, you may
need to place something under
your napkins when stamping so
the paint doesn't bleed through
and onto your work surface.

a

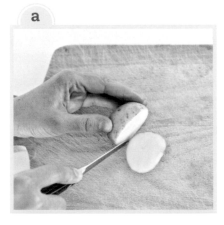

b

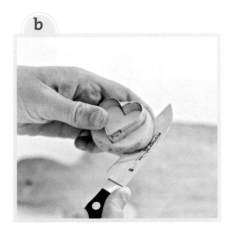

c

d

e

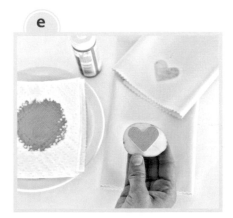

Dessert Flags

Adding flags to the dessert table not only lets people know the names of each item, but it also creates a warm, homemade feel fitting for a Farm Chicks wedding. The flag "poles" are wooden stir sticks, which can be inexpensively purchased in large quantities at restaurant supply stores and food warehouses. These instructions make approximately nine flags.

what you'll need

2 pieces of fabric, 10 inches (25.4 cm) square

1 piece of double-sided fusible web, 10 inches (25.4 cm) square

Iron

Paper cutter (optional)

Scissors

Small letter rubber stamps and inkpad, or black fine-point marker

¼-inch (6 mm) bias tape or ribbon: 4-inch (10.2 cm) strips for each flag

Wooden stir sticks

Hot glue gun and glue sticks

Sharp craft knife

what you do

1 Place the two fabric squares with wrong sides together. Remove the paper backing from the fusible web and sandwich it between the two pieces of fabric. Press the layers together with an iron, following the manufacturer's directions for the fusible web. ⓐ

2 Use scissors or a paper cutter to cut the fused fabric into 2½-inch (6.4 cm) strips. ⓑ

3 Cut the strips into thirds so that each piece measures 3½ x 2½ inches (8.9 x 6.4 cm). Use scissors to cut a triangular notch on one short side of each fabric piece to complete the flag shape.

4 Stamp (or handwrite with a marker) dessert names onto bias tape, making sure that the word will fit the length of the flag. Cut the bias tape to fit the flag. Affix the bias tape onto the flag using a hot glue gun. ⓒ

5 Cut two slits into the flags with a sharp craft knife to weave the stir sticks through. Flip the flag over and hot glue the flag to the stick with a tiny dot of glue.

a

b

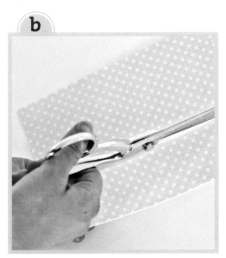

c

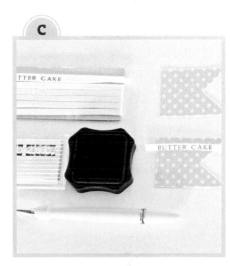

Farm Bucket
cake stand

For a truly eye-catching dessert table, vary the heights of each sweet by using stands, crates, and plates. This unique cake stand begins with an old pail from the farm, adding charm and personality to a classic dish.

what you'll need

Galvanized bucket
Hammer
Plate
Rubber dots (optional)

what you do

1 Wash and dry the bucket.
2 Remove the handle, if necessary, and pound down side handle-holders with a hammer. ⓐ ⓑ
3 Turn the bucket upside-down and place the cake plate on top. If you'd like a more secure cake stand, affix rubber dots to the bottom of the plate. ⓒ ⓓ

ⓐ

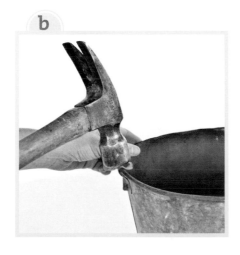

ⓑ

ⓒ

ⓓ

Homemade Cakes

Nothing says "farm wedding" more than old-fashioned homemade cakes displayed on pretty cake plates. A large butter cake with a sweet glaze and fresh fruit, a layered crepe cake, and individual Bundt cakes with fruit and powdered sugar can help set a colorful and delicious food table.

BUTTER CAKE

butter cake recipe

what you'll need

Mixing bowls
Measuring cups and spoons
Beater
Bundt cake pan
Oven
Whisk
Microwave oven

CAKE

1 cup butter
2 cups sugar
4 eggs
1 teaspoon vanilla
3 cups flour, sifted
½ teaspoon baking soda
½ teaspoon baking powder
½ teaspoon salt
1 cup buttermilk

GLAZE

2 tablespoons butter
2 tablespoons milk
2 teaspoons vanilla
2 cups powdered sugar

what you do

1 Preheat oven to 325°F. Cream butter and sugar until light and fluffy. Add egg one at a time, beating well after each. Add vanilla and beat until well combined.

2 Sift dry ingredients together and add alternately with buttermilk. Beat for 3 minutes at medium speed. Do not over-beat or your cake will fall.

3 Pour batter into prepared Bundt cake pan and bake for approximately 1 hour, or until toothpick inserted comes out clean.

4 While the cake is baking, prepare the glaze. Add butter and milk to bowl and heat in microwave until butter is melted (about 30 seconds). Add vanilla and powdered sugar and whisk until smooth. Spoon over cooled butter cake, allowing big drips all around the cake.

Orange Juice
rosemary sippers

Signature drinks are fun to have at a wedding—they're a memorable, festive way to carry out the theme. Because The Farm Chicks wedding has a breakfast theme, this drink has an orange juice base, with a sprig of rosemary for garnish. Look for rosemary plants in the spring and summer at nurseries or a home improvement store's garden section, or look for rosemary trees in December as a seasonal item.

what you'll need

Large vessel or pitcher

Orange juice

Club soda

Cointreau (optional)

Rosemary sprigs

what you do

1 Pour orange juice and club soda into the vessel at a ratio of 3 cups of orange juice to 1 cup of club soda and stir. Add in a splash of Cointreau, if desired, and stir.

2 Serve by ladling or pouring the drink into glasses. Garnish each glass with a rosemary sprig, which doubles as a swizzle stick.

Swizzle Sticks

Swizzle sticks add a carefree festive touch to any drink. You can use long twigs, branches, or herbs, such as the rosemary sprig, but if you'd like the sticks to look more uniform, here's an idea: Gather wooden sticks or dowels. Wrap the top of each stick with ribbon and tie it at the top. Trim the edge of the ribbon, leaving a few inches to hang down.

Milk with Paper Straws

It's a great idea to have ice-cold milk on hand at the wedding reception, for guests to enjoy with homemade cakes and treats. Fill individual-sized milk jars, either vintage or upcycled coffee beverage jars, with regular and chocolate varieties. Topping them with colorful paper straws is a fun way to present this yummy and nutritious beverage. Place the jars in a galvanized metal bucket packed with ice to keep everything cold and inviting.

Tea Bag
takeaways

For a sweet favor, set up a table with various tea choices and let guests fill up their own muslin tea bags—found inexpensively online—with their preference. To create the tags, find your favorite fabric and make a paper copy of it. This adds a fun, unexpected texture to the paper and incorporates a country feel for the take-home gift.

what you'll need

Muslin tea bags, each 2½ x 4 inches (6.4 x 10.2 cm)

White cardstock, 8½ x 11 inches (21.6 x 27.98 cm)

1 piece of patterned fabric, slightly larger than 8½ x 11 inches (21.6 x 28 cm)

Color copy machine

2½-inch (6.4 cm) scallop-shaped hole punch

Letter stamps and inkpad or a fine-point marker

Tiny hole punch

what you do

1 Place the fabric into a copier, with the right side facing the glass. Make copies onto cardstock. With the 2½-inch (6.4 cm) scallop-shaped hole punch, you can make 12 tags from one sheet of cardstock, so calculate what you'll need for your number of guests.

2 Punch out scallop shapes from the copied cardstock. (a) (b)

3 Stamp or handwrite messages onto tags. (c)

4 Use a tiny hole punch to make a hole at the top of each tag. Using the string on the muslin bag, tie the tags onto the bags. (d)

a

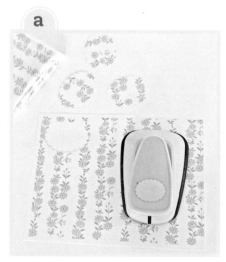

b

c

d

A Favored Table Display

Find an antique cart to house your tea bag takeaway station. Gather jars and scoops for each of the teas, as well as a small box for the muslin bags. The tea bag takeaway station, set off to the side of the event, will provide welcome entertainment for guests while not distracting from the main affair.

Natural and Organic wedding

with Minna Mercke Schmidt

www.blomsterverkstad.com

These wedding projects, styled by Minna Mercke Schmidt, will inspire anyone who believes that flowers are the true essence of romance. With an organic, delicate vibe and plenty of feminine details, this nature-based wedding is both beautiful and relaxed. Gathered plant life from the roadside and farmers' markets combine with stunning glass jars and unique vases to create a breathtaking work of vegetable and flower art, sure to instill romance, hope, and a sense of new beginnings.

natural, approachable arrangements

Nature really was the highlight of this wedding, and not just the flowers—in fact, vegetables, herbs, and all manner of greenery were just as important for this organic event. Minna has always strived to look for the beauty in everyday items, so she pulled together a variety of common plants for these wedding projects. From cabbage leaves and artichokes on the tables to asparagus and berries in the centerpieces, an inventive use of all kinds of plants was seen in every aspect of the décor. Minna even created a "cake" out of roses, fruits, and herbs—a stunning display of earth's creations.

Minna's Simple Ways to Cut Costs

- Use common vegetables in addition to, or in place of, flowers.
- Look for the beauty in everyday natural elements, such as eggshells, rocks, and moss.
- Be inventive when it comes to repurposing. A dry cleaning hanger can become a wreath, apples on the ground can become décor—even leftover cabbage leaves can become part of the tablescape!

Minna's goal for the centerpieces, table settings, and displays was to create something beautiful but not stiff. She knew that if everything looked too perfect, people would be afraid to touch, admire, or even go near the tables. To achieve this approachable feeling, she arranged the flowers in a more organic way, with cascading vines and simple garden pots. Juxtaposed against the awe-inspiring arrangements were wooden clothespins and lengths of jute string—simple touches that added a down-to-earth feel.

a perfectly pale backdrop for beauty

So as to not distract from the flowers and vegetables, Minna relied on pale colors and simple furniture to complete the displays. Antique tables and wicker chairs provided a textural backdrop for the vegetation, while pale pinks, greens, and creamy whites could be seen in the furniture, tulle, and ribbons.

By blending awe-inspiring floral and vegetable arrangements with clever uses of everyday items, Minna created a fresh, natural stage perfect for a lovely, classic wedding.

Flower Wreath
with hanger

An inexpensive metal clothes hanger forms the foundation for this wreath. Make sure you have plenty of material to fill your wreath before you get started—you don't want to have to stop working to go fetch more materials, and you also run the risk of not being able to find the same flowers again. You can buy flowers at your local farmers' market, but also look for wildflowers or even weeds near your home—they can be just as beautiful and can give a more natural, carefree vibe to an arrangement.

what you'll need

1 metal clothes hanger
Needle-nose pliers
Assorted floral material such as small flowers, wildflowers, greenery, and weeds to make approximately 20 small bouquets
Spool of thin 24-gauge metal wire
Wire cutters

what you do

1 Form the metal clothes hanger into the shape of a heart by using your hands and needle-nose pliers. ⓐ

2 Use your floral material to make a small bouquet with short stalks, and wrap the ends with a piece of thin metal wire. Repeat this process until you have made approximately 20 small bouquets.

3 Attach the bouquets to the hanger with the thin wire, spinning the wire around the hanger as you go. Arrange the bouquets in a fishbone pattern: one angling to the left, then one angling to the right, and so on. Place each new bouquet on top of the previous one's stalks so you don't see anything but flowers. ⓑ

4 Make additional bouquets if needed, and continue attaching them to the hanger until the wreath is complete. You may be able to hang the wreath using the original wire, but use the thin wire for extra enforcement or a loop at the top, as needed.

Artichoke Décor

Artichokes are beautiful plants that look so intriguing on their own that you don't need to dress them up to have them work as decorations. Look for big, blossoming artichokes, and place them directly on the table in an artful manner. The same goes for interesting heads of lettuce, including small Brussels sprouts.

Love Seeds

Small, personal favors are always popular. Keep it simple—and useful—by spreading seeds of love. The seeds could be your favorite flower, herb, or vegetable. If you decide on a more complicated plant, consider including instructions for how to plant and take care of the seeds. Hang the favors on a clothesline or chicken wire display for a cute decorative element.

what you'll need

Thick brown paper, 8 inches
(20.3 cm) square

Decorative-edged scissors

Heart-shaped metal brad

Inkpads in assorted colors

Letter stamps and decorative
rubber stamp

Seeds, approximately 1 teaspoon

Baker's twine, 12 inches
(30.5 cm) long

*The supplies listed are for one
favor; collect what you need
for your event.*

what you do

1 Lay the paper on a flat surface
diagonally so that one corner
of the paper is pointing toward
you. Fold that corner up to meet
the opposite corner so that the
paper looks like a triangle.

2 Fold in the left point across to
the opposite straight edge until
they meet, and press the paper
flat with your fingers. Fold the
right point across the folded left
point to the opposite straight
edge and press flat.

3 Open the envelope on the top
and cut the top edges with
decorative-edged scissors. Fold
the front flap down and secure
it with a brad pushed through to
the inside of the envelope.

4 Decorate the outside of the
envelope using letter stamps
and a decorative stamp, with
inkpads in assorted colors.

5 Pour seeds into the envelope,
and then fold down the back flap
and tuck it into the envelope.

6 Finish by threading a length of
string under the front envelope
flap and tying the ends together.

love seeds

Presentation

If you would like the favors to serve double duty as place cards, add a personalized, handwritten tag to each envelope. Alternatively, tie a piece of clothesline somewhere at your event, use clothespins to display the favors, and invite each guest to choose one to take home at the end of the event.

Rose and Cabbage Vase Garlands

For a unique, fresh take on garlands, suspend a section of clothesline somewhere at your event. Then use clothespins to hold up mini cabbage vases filled with roses. To make a cabbage vase, carefully roll a piece of savoy cabbage into a thin cone shape and use floral wire to hold it in place. Stuff the vase with a piece of soaking wet paper towel before tucking a flower into it.

chicken wire *Heart*

Wrapping chicken wire around moss is a clever and, easy way to add fun shapes and a touch of green to your wedding décor. Moss is a particularly smart solution for fall and winter weddings, when some flowers may be harder to come by. Keep the moss bright and moist by spritzing it with water from a spray bottle and keeping it out of direct sunlight.

what you'll need

- 1 piece of chicken wire: 6 x 7 inches (15.2 x 17.8 cm)
- 1 piece of moss, slightly smaller than the chicken wire
- Safety gloves
- 2 pieces of thin 24-gauge metal wire:
  - 10 inches (25.4 cm) long
  - 18 inches (45.7 cm) long
- Wire cutters
- 1 piece of heavy 16-gauge metal wire (see step 3 for length)
- Needle-nose pliers
- 12 small pearl beads
- Clay or craft dough, approximately 1 cup (8 ounces)
- Small planter pot

what you do

1. Lay the chicken wire on a flat surface and cover it with moss. Place the moss facedown, so the good side is facing the wire and the flat surface. Wearing safety gloves, fold the chicken wire up on all sides so it covers the moss and slightly overlaps. Secure the chicken wire with the shorter piece of thin metal wire by weaving it in and out of the chicken wire. Trim excess with wire cutters.
2. Press and shape the moss and wire into a heart with your hands. (a)
3. Press the piece of 16-gauge metal wire through the bottom of the heart, pushing it all the way through the moss until it comes through the other side. This wire will be the heart's stem, which holds the heart up in a planter pot. Adjust the height of the wire depending on how tall you'd like your heart to stand. Twist the wire at the top of the heart into a small rounded shape using needle-nose pliers. (b)
4. Thread a small pearl bead onto the longer piece of thin wire and twist to secure. Repeat until all beads are threaded and secured, spacing them approximately 1 to 2 inches (2.5 to 5.1 cm) from each other. Twist the wire onto the stem and heart to hold everything in place.
5. Press the clay into a small planter pot. (c)
6. Stick the wire stem into the clay, adding moss to cover the clay.

a

b

c

Parsley in Cabbage Pot

When you begin to see everyday vegetables as viable options for wedding décor, the possibilities are endless. For example, a simple pot of parsley can add a touch of greenery and interesting texture to a tablescape. For added appeal, wrap the pot with a large piece of cabbage and bind it with jute string or twine.

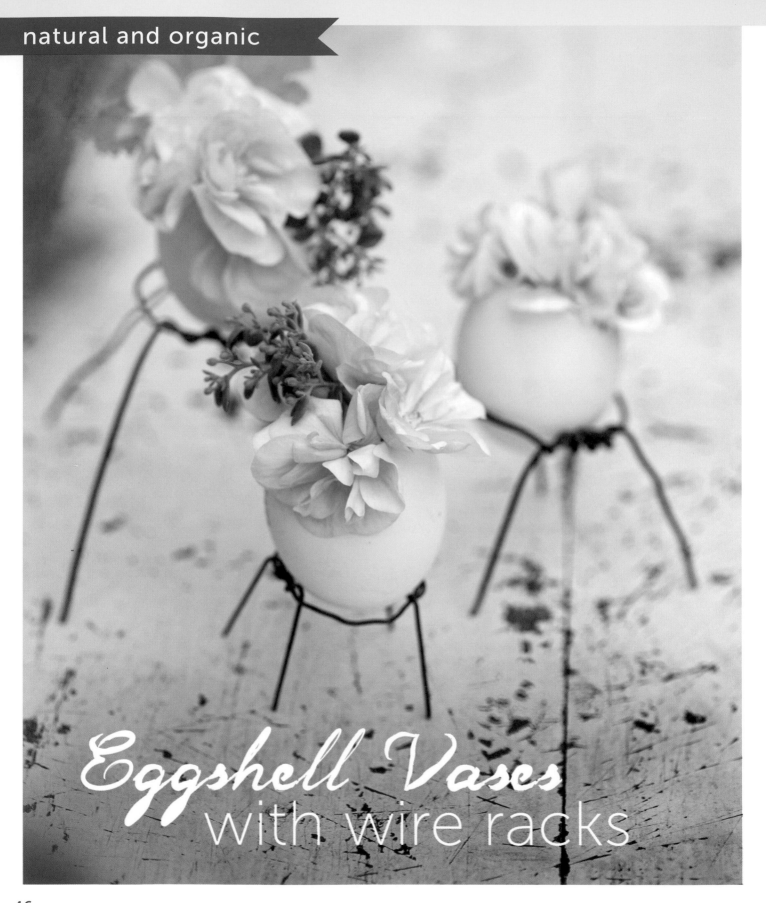

Eggshell Vases
with wire racks

Vases don't need to be made out of glass or china. Inventively using items from nature adds another level of organic beauty. The trick to using eggshells is to crack them a little higher than halfway up on the egg. This will make the vase as stable as possible. It may take some experimenting to get the legs and eggshells in just the right position to stand on their own, but the eye-catching end result is well worth the effort.

what you'll need

Egg
Sharp kitchen knife
2 pieces of thick 16-gauge metal wire
   as follows:
   • 6 inches (15.2 cm) long
   • 7 inches (17.8 cm) long
Wire cutters
Water
Delicate flower and greenery

what you do

1 Crack the top portion of an egg with a blunt metal edge like a sharp kitchen knife. Remove a few small parts of the shell at the cracked top and empty out the egg. Rinse out the empty eggshell with water and let dry.

2 In roughly the center of the longer piece of wire, wrap the shorter piece of wire as shown. Leave approximately 1½ inches (3.8 cm) of unwrapped wire at the ends of the short wire, pointing in the same direction, to serve as the first two legs of the vase stand. ⓐ

3 Shape the longer piece of wire into a circle, leaving two long ends to twist into two more legs. ⓑ

4 Use wire cutters to cut the legs to equal lengths, so the rack is stable.

5 Set the eggshell on top of the stand. Gently fill the eggshell with water and add a delicate flower and greenery.

a

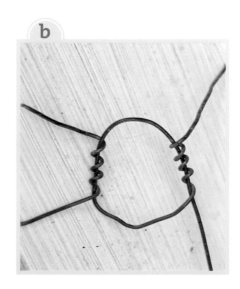
b

Asparagus bouquet

Vegetables with interesting forms and textures and can be just as attractive as flowers. Plus, they're often a less expensive way to add natural elements into the décor. Look for the freshest stalks of asparagus you can find for these bouquets. The fresher they are, the greener they'll be and the easier time they'll have standing up straight.

what you'll need

8 to 10 thick stalks of asparagus
Rubber band
Burlap or jute fabric, 12 x 3 inches
   (30.5 x 7.6 cm)
Jute string, 18 inches (45.7 cm) long
Sharp kitchen knife

what you do

1 Gather the asparagus into a small bouquet, with all stalks pointing the same direction. Put a rubber band around the bouquet to hold the bunch in place. (a)

2 Wrap the burlap or jute fabric around the asparagus, allowing it to overlap a bit. Then wrap the jute string around the fabric and tie a bow to secure. (b)

3 To ensure the bouquet will stand on its own, trim the bottom of the stalks with a sharp kitchen knife so that they are level.

4 Repeat these steps to make the number of bouquets needed for your event. If you are making the bouquets more than 24 hours in advance, store them on a shallow platter or pan filled with about 1 inch (2.5 cm) of water.

a

b

Flower and Vegetable cake

The cake is a central element in any wedding. "Baking" a pretty decorative cake, with materials from your garden and the local farmers' market, shows that simple ingredients from nature can make unbelievable beauty. Two foam blocks—the kind used in floral arranging—comprise the base of this cake. The key to a successful cake is letting the blocks soak up the water at their own pace, to ensure there's enough moisture for the flowers.

what you'll need

2 floral foam blocks, 9 x 4 x 3 inches (22.9 x 10.2 x 7.6 cm)

Bucket filled with water

Cake stand

Sharp floral knife

4 pieces of thick 16-gauge metal wire, each 7 inches (17.8 cm) long

Wire cutters

Large rubber band

60 to 65 stalks of rye grass, each approximately 5 inches (12.7 cm) tall

12 roses in two shades of pink

Small, fresh greeneries, such as oregano leaves and currant berries

Jute string, approximately 60 inches (152.4 cm) long

Scissors

what you do

1 Place the two foam blocks in the bucket and let them soak up water until they are heavy and sink to the bottom. Place the saturated blocks on your cake stand with two long sides abutting. Cut each of the outer edges into a half moon to form a cake shape. ⓐ

2 Secure the two blocks by opening up the half moons, sticking the 4 wires into the flat sides, and pressing the blocks back together.

3 Stretch the rubber band all the way around the cake form to further secure it. Insert upright stalks of rye grass beneath the rubber band, all the way around the cake form. ⓑ

4 Cut the roses with a sharp floral knife and stick them into the top of the foam block. Once the large flowers are in place, fill in the rest of the space with fresh greeneries and berries. Lastly, tie the jute string around the cake and make a bow to secure. Cut and remove the rubber band. ⓒ

Seasonal Preferences

When selecting flowers and vegetables for your cake and the rest of the décor, it's best to choose according to what's in season. Roses in shades of pink were used here, accented with currant berries and oregano, but any flower will work for this arrangement. Experiment with a variety of seasonal favorites, according to your preferences and color scheme, until you find a pleasing arrangement for your "cake."

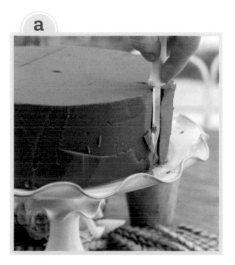

a

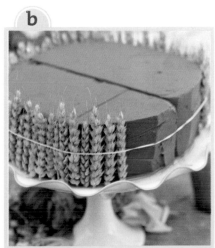

b

c

Vintage Glam
wedding

with Tiffany Kirchner-Dixon

www.thefancyfarmgirl.com

This wedding features old Hollywood glamour, a black-and-white color scheme with pops of pink and glitter, and vintage goodness in every corner. Tiffany Kirchner-Dixon created these wedding projects by balancing repurposed vintage items with a classically clean color scheme and a touch of pure fanciness throughout.

fancy, classic colors

The sleek color combination of white, black, and light pink—highlighted with silvers, golds, and glitters—sets the stage in this movie-worthy event. A white satin dress, accented with a bold black ribbon, adorned the bride and was paired with fun vintage black-and-white shoes. The same color scheme was echoed in the tablescapes to provide consistency. This basic palette allowed the unique colors hidden throughout the décor to really pop—for example, the bright colors on the glass bottle labels, the hints of color in the vintage train case card keeper, and the peach tints seen in some of the vintage décor. The beautiful light pinks also stood out against the black satin to create a striking display.

If you're aiming for a specific color scheme, simple is better. For example, white, black, and light pink help this entire event look cohesive and gorgeous.

Tiffany's Simple Ways to Cut Costs

- Use small bottles as vases, which lets you use floral arrangements of only one or two flowers.
- Repurpose old photo frames, lampshades, and suitcases in your décor.
- Dress up your cake stand inexpensively with wrapping paper.

Tiffany's Ingredients for a Terrific Wedding

- A cohesive mood, where the food, lighting, music, and décor all work together
- Just the right scale—not too many people, but not too few
- A happy, relaxed attitude from the bride and groom, wedding party, and all involved

dazzling lights of old hollywood

Rhinestones, crystals, and black-and-white photographs blended into the color scheme well while adding texture and interest. A repurposed lampshade was dressed up and hung over the tables to make each guest feel like they were at a fancy dinner party. With just one or two flowers in each vase, Tiffany was free to create arrangements with several vases instead of just one. This allowed the vases to become an eye-catching part of the tablescape themselves, rather than just a vessel hidden by flowers.

Tiffany loves re-creating the glamorous events and lifestyles of the past, and what better time than to do it than for a wedding? With a vintage-inspired hairpiece and faux fur cape, a dazzling sign with big twinkle lights, and a dash of romantic music, the bride and groom could be on their way to see a picture show in the 1940s—or a fabulous party, just for them.

Hollywood Light frame

Tiffany was inspired by the famous premier signs of old Hollywood movies for this project. There's something so glamorous and exciting about big flashing twinkle lights! For the inside of the frame, you could have a photograph, or follow Tiffany's lead and create a chalkboard. It's the perfect canvas for adding your own creative stamp to the wedding décor.

what you'll need

Large vintage frame, with sides at
    least 2 inches (5.1 cm) wide
Tape measure
Strand of umbrella lights with globe
    bulbs
Black permanent marker
Wire cutters
Drill bit and drill
Scrap wood block
Staple gun and staples

what you do

1 To arrange the lights evenly around the frame, measure the length and width of the frame, and then count the sockets on the strand. Measure and mark out the bulb spacing with a permanent marker. (a)

2 If the sockets have umbrella clips, use wire cutters with a cutting edge to remove them. (b)

3 Choose a drill bit slightly larger than the socket width, so that when you drill the frame, the socket can slide into the hold. Using a scrap wood block as backing for the frame, center the drill tip in each mark and carefully drill a hole from the front side of the frame through to the back.

You may need an assistant to hold the frame to keep it from moving while drilling. (c)

4 Remove the bulbs from the sockets and, starting at the bottom corner of the frame, push the socket closest to the cord end through the back of the frame. Carefully centering the staples over the cord (you do NOT want to puncture the cord), staple the cord to the frame on either side of the socket. Repeat with each socket. (d) .

5 Secure excess cord with more staples, or use tie wraps to tie excess cord together. (e)

6 Screw in the bulbs and plug in the lights. (f)

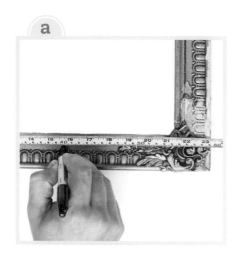

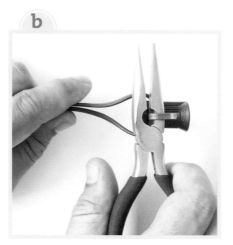

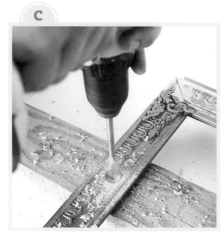

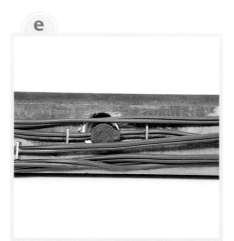

Oh Happy Day

To make a chalkboard, cut a piece of Masonite board to the dimensions of the frame. Spray the Masonite with several coats of black chalkboard spray paint. Let dry. Place the painted board into the frame and use chalk to write a message for the guests.

Bride and Groom Chair Monograms

Monograms add an extra special touch to the bride and groom's dining chairs. If you can't find existing chipboard letters, use a stencil to create your own. With a little glue, glitter, and some black ribbon to hang it, you're set!

Train Case Card Keeper

For a unique take on a card box, use an antique train case. Decorate it with vintage Hollywood photos, feathers, and flower petals, and make a sign that says "Cards" for easy access for guests.

Repurposed
Chandelier

This crystal chandelier relies on a repurposed lampshade for its base, so look for a boned lampshade at your local thrift store. This is a fast way to add light and shine to your wedding; once the event is over, use it to fancy up your bedroom or bathroom! If you'd rather not worry about finding a light cord kit, simply attach chain lengths to the top of the shade and hang it. It won't light up, but it will still make an impact. You could even make one for each dinner table and add a glittered number to help guests find their seats.

what you'll need

Small lampshade

1½-inch-wide (3.8 cm) black ribbon:
- approximately 3 yards (2.7 m) to cover the lampshade
- 7 to 10 pieces for the bows, each 12 inches (30.5 cm) long

Scissors

Wire cutters

6 pieces of 20-gauge wire, each 18 inches (845.7 cm) long

Small glass vases with necks, all the same size

Light cord kit

Low wattage light bulb

Crystal chain

Crystal drops

Water

Fresh flowers

what you do

1 Remove all the fabric covering the lampshade. On the lampshade skeleton, tie a small knot on the bottom rim and begin to weave the ribbon at an angle, up to the top rim and back down again. Distribute the ribbon equally around the shade. When finished, tie a small knot at the end of the ribbon, securing it tightly to the

shade. Trim excess ribbon with scissors. ⓐ

2 Tie bows around the lampshade at the base of every other ribbon (or every ribbon, if you prefer). ⓑ

3 Wrap half of a wire length tightly around the neck of the vase, leaving the other half to secure the vase to the bottom rim of the shade. Twist over the wire ends to tightly secure

them. Adjust the bottle to hang upright so it will hold water and flowers. Attach a vase at every junction of the shade, to ensure the lampshade will be equally weighted and hang straight. ⓒ

4 Attach the light cord kit to the lampshade following the cord kit directions.

5 Attach crystal chain so it will drape and swag equally between

each vase. If it's not secure enough, use a small lengths of wire to wrap it securely to the shade as needed. ⓓ

6 Add a crystal drop in the middle of each chain loop. ⓔ

7 Fill the vases with water and fresh flowers, then hang the chandelier and plug it in! ⓕ

a

b

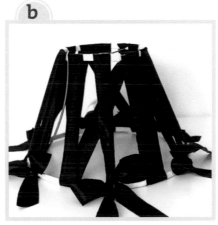

c

d

e

f

Pretty as a Package
cake stand

A package wrapped with black-and-white damask paper serves as a stand for the cake—instant glam for very little money! Tiffany also incorporated the color scheme by resting fluffy pink flowers on each layer of the cake. If you want to display more than one dessert, you can wrap several different size packages to create varying heights. Either way, make sure each box is larger than the bottom of the dessert and sturdy enough to hold the weight of the sweet.

what you'll need

Sturdy papier-mâché or wood box with lid slightly larger than your cake
Double-sided tape
Scissors
Black-and-white damask wrapping paper
2-inch-wide (5.1 cm) silver ribbon, long enough to wrap around the box

1-inch-wide (2.5 cm) black velvet ribbon, long enough to wrap around the box and make a bow
2-tier cake (optional)
10 to 12 floral water tubes (optional)
10 to 12 pink flowers, with stems trimmed short to fit into water tubes (optional)

what you do

1 Remove the lid from the box. Line the inside edges of the box close to the top with double-sided tape, leaving the backing on for now.

2 Place the box in the center of the wrapping paper and cut a piece large enough to cover the entire box and fold into the top by at least 1 inch (2.5 cm).

3 Cut a piece of double-sided tape and place it on the bottom of the box. Secure the box to the center of paper so it will not move while you are working with it. Make a diagonal cut from each corner of the paper to the nearest corner of the box. ⓐ

4 Remove the backing on the tape inside the box. Fold the paper up to the top of the box and over the edge, securing it with the tape. ⓑ

5 Trim the paper "wings" if they are too large to fit inside the box. ⓒ Continue all the way around the box, and repeat all the steps with the lid. Place lid on box.

6 Repeat steps 1–5 to cover the lid of the box, then place the lid on box.

7 Wrap the silver ribbon all the way around the box and secure it with double-sided tape. Wrap the black ribbon on top of the silver ribbon and tie it in a bow in the front. ⓓ

8 Place the cake on top of the box. Place flowers in the cake using floral water tubes. Remove the tubes when it is time to serve the cake.

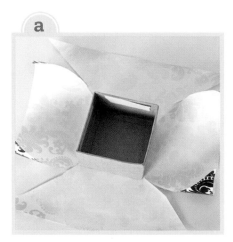

ⓐ

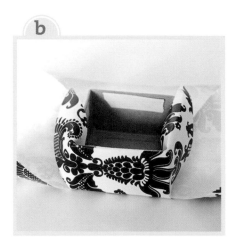

ⓑ

ⓒ

ⓓ

Galvanized
favor tins

Tiffany created these tins so that each wedding guest would have a daily reminder to "remember the love" of the happy couple's special day. It's a favor that keeps on giving, and is sure to be appreciated by every attendee. The galvanized metal tags are easy to make, inexpensive, and adds a unique touch of glamour.

what you'll need

Thin galvanized metal sheets cut into
  1¾ x ½ inch (4.4 x 1.3 cm) strips

Scrap wood block

Steel ⅛-inch (0.3 cm) letter stamping
  kit (available at hardware stores)

Ball peen hammer

Black patina

Paintbrush

Old rag or cloth

Steel wool

Pliers

Small metal tins*

Industrial-strength glue

Love quotes printed on paper and
  cut into strips

Tin snips

* Available at container stores
   or kitchen supply stores. The
   ones shown here are vintage
   tins, approximately 2 inches
   (5.1 cm) tall.

what you do

1 Place a metal strip on top of
   a scrap wood block. Plan out
   where the letters of the word
   need to be fit on the strip, then
   line up the first metal letter
   stamp where you want your
   word to begin. Hold the stamp
   securely and hit the top once
   very hard with the ball peen
   hammer, making sure not to
   move the stamp as you're hitting
   it. Continue lining up letters and
   repeating this step until your
   word is complete. ⓐ

2 Paint a thick layer of black
   patina over the metal-stamped
   word and allow it to sit for 2–5
   minutes. ⓑ ⓒ

3 With an old cloth or rag, wipe
   the metal piece clean. Gently
   rub the stamped piece with steel
   wool to remove excess black,
   being careful not to rub the
   patina off of the word.

4 Using pliers, gently shape the
   metal-stamped word to fit a
   round tin. Glue the word to the
   tin using industrial-strength
   glue and allow it to dry
   overnight. ⓓ

5 Fold and place strips of love
   quote strips inside the tins.

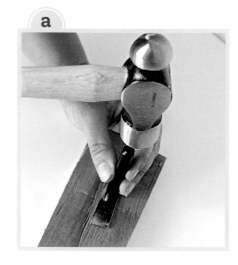

a

b

c

d

Vintage Glam
capelette

Hollywood actresses from the 1940s always seemed to have extravagant feather boas and fur capes. This simple, faux version gives the same vibe, and it adds a layer of warmth for a fall or winter wedding. Borrow a vintage brooch from someone special to you, such as a grandmother, to secure this capelette on your special day.

what you'll need

Measuring tape

Faux fur

Satin or other fabric for lining

Scissors

Pins

Sewing machine

Thread

Needle (optional)

Vintage brooch

what you do

1 To determine the size of the capelette, do the following:
   - For the length: Wrap a measuring tape loosely around your body, allowing it to fall around each shoulder and meet in the middle of the chest. Note the measurement and add 2 inches (5.1 cm) for seam allowance. ⓐ
   - For the width: Wrap a shawl or scarf around you and fold it as needed to test what width you want the capelette to be. (The finished capelette shown is about 12 inches (30.5 cm) wide.) Add 1 inch (2.5 cm) to the desired finished width, for two seam allowances.

2 Cut one piece of fur and one piece of satin according to your dimensions. ⓑ

3 Pin the satin and fur together, with the right sides facing each other. ⓒ

4 Sew the fabrics together using a straight stitch, leaving approximately 10 inches (25.4 cm) unsewn on one side for turning the fabrics right side out. ⓓ

5 Trim the corners and turn the fabrics right side out through the opening. Use the eraser end of a pencil or your finger to push out the corners. ⓔ Hand-sew or machine-stitch the opening closed, and trim all loose threads.

6 Use a vintage brooch to pin the capelette together.

a

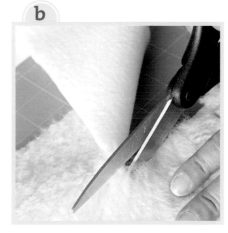

b

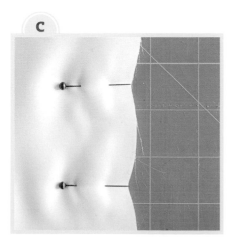

c

d

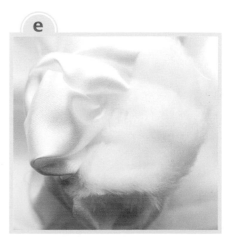

e

Romantic
and pretty wedding

www.heatherbullard.com

If decades-old photographs, trinkets, and decorations tug at your heartstrings, then this romantic wedding designed by Heather Bullard may be just the inspiration for your special event. With a sophisticated eye for vintage beauties and a talent for combining pretty elements, Heather turned to antiques, family heirlooms, and a classically clean color palette for her wedding projects.

classic romance

Family heirlooms and photographs add significance to these delicate, pretty projects, as they whisper of a true love that has survived the test of time. Heather gathered wedding photos, antique vases and dishes, and vintage fabrics from family members and local thrift stores in anticipation of the event. She photocopied family wedding photos to act as tags on which guests could write their well wishes for the happy couple. Vintage postcards served as focal points for the centerpieces, adding another layer of history to the setting.

Vintage fabrics and embellishments also played a part. A sentimental handkerchief wrapped in an elegant piece of silk and held in place with an antique family brooch encompassed the bouquet, allowing the bride to carry a piece of her past down the aisle. Heather also used vintage linens and ribbons in the dining table décor as napkins and embellishments. Including family heirlooms and vintage items allows for a deeper sense of romance and commitment, as a clear indication of the families and stories that join together on this special day.

pretty in pastel

Juxtaposed against the antique items and family heirlooms, pastel hues and soft flowers lent a modern, airy feel to the scene. White table linens provided a blank canvas for not only the vintage china place settings, but also the pretty flowers in shades of sage green, soft pink, and warm cream. Painted tissue paper lanterns in shades of pastel blues, pinks, and sparkly gold hung low above the tables, while gifts wrapped in vintage paper festively filled wire baskets. Kraft boxes, painted in pastel tones and filled with Jordan almonds in matching colors, further accentuated the feminine color palette. With delicate fabrics, beautiful colors, and sentimental photos, you'll have a romantic, pretty wedding that can't be beat.

Heather's Simple Ways to Cut Costs
- Incorporate as many handmade elements as possible
- Reuse sentimental family photos and heirlooms

Heather's Advice For Newlyweds

Consider each other your best friend. Compromise. Learn to pick your battles. Always believe the best in each other. And try to treat each other kindly on a daily basis.

Colorful treat boxes

A simple kraft box can be transformed to fit the theme of any wedding, and it's the perfect size to fill with small treats to thank your guests for being part of your wedding day.

what you'll need

Small kraft box: 2¼ x 3 x 1 inches
   (5.7 x 7.6 x 2.5 cm)
Craft paints in assorted colors,
   including shimmery gold
Foam brush
Paper cup and water for
   rinsing brush
Paper towel
Tissue paper: 9 x 3 inches
   (22.9 x 7.6 cm)
Candies of choice
9 inches (22.9 cm) of velvet ribbon,
   ⅜ inch (.95 cm) wide
Hot glue gun and glue stick
Millinery flowers
Ribbons
Embellishments of choice
Glue gun

what you do

1 Paint the bottom of the box with gold craft paint and foam brush. Rinse the brush in water, and dab it on a paper towel to dry.

2 Paint the box lid with a different color of craft paint and foam brush. Rinse the brush. Let the box and lid dry.

3 Apply a very light coat of gold paint to the painted lid to add a hint of sheen. Let dry. Rinse the brush and let dry. ⓐ

4 Line the box with tissue paper and fill it with your favorite candies. ⓑ

5 Fold over left and right sides of the tissue so they overlap. Place the lid on the box.

6 Wrap velvet ribbon lengthwise around the middle of the box, and secure with a hot glue gun.

7 Attach a vintage millinery flower to the top of the box with a hot glue gun. ⓒ

Favors for the VIPs

Use larger boxes to make gifts that stand out for VIPs to make them feel special. Simply start with a larger-sized kraft box and cut tissue paper to fit the larger box. You can also use thicker ribbon and larger millinery flowers.

a

b

c

A Touch of Silk

To instantly dress up the place settings, wrap linen napkins with strips of velvet. Found by the yard at fabric stores or in bins at antique stores, silk ribbon used even in small amounts adds a touch of luxury.

Old, New, Borrowed,
and blue bouquet

Use family heirlooms, or perhaps even mementos from the bride and groom's courtship, to make this bouquet all the more meaningful. Dressing up the bouquet is also a chance to infuse more of your style and color into the event. And, if you're clever, you could manage to incorporate "something old, something new, something borrowed, and something blue" all in this one small but important item.

what you'll need

Bridal bouquet (handmade or from a florist)

Vintage hankie (something old)

Jewelry charm (something new)

Antique brooch (something borrowed)

1 yard (.9 m) of vintage ribbon, 3 inches (7.62 cm) wide (something blue)

5–7 floral pins

what you do

1 Wrap the bouquet with the ribbon and secure it with floral pins. **a**

2 Tuck the hankie into a fold of the ribbon and let part of it peek out from the bottom. **b**

3 Attach the jewelry charm with a floral pin to the bouquet, making sure to pin it through both the ribbon and the top of the hankie to secure it. **c**

4 Attach the vintage brooch above the jewelry charm. **d**

Place Cards

For a refined place card, handwrite each guest's name on a small piece of white paper and slip it into a metal tag holder. You can find assorted types of metal tag holders in office supply, craft, and online stores. Or look for vintage ones at flea markets and on eBay auctions. Wrap the tag around a small bunch of flowers with a ribbon for guests to enjoy.

Paper Lantern bundle

Simple white paper lanterns are easy to find in stores and online these days, but what's even greater is the range of colors available in spray paint and craft paint. You're sure to find the right color for your event. For this romantic affair, Heather used gold, dusty pink, and pale blue to cover her lanterns. Use lanterns in a variety of sizes and shapes for a dramatic effect.

what you'll need

3 paper lanterns in assorted sizes
Foam brush
Blue and pink craft paint
Paper cup and water for rinsing brush
Paper towel
Gold spray paint
Assorted ephemera such as streamers, ribbons, and millinery flowers
24-gauge craft wire
Scissors

what you do

1 Unfold the paper lanterns to paint them. For the blue and pink lanterns, paint the desired color with a foam brush. If you're working with two different colors of paint at once, be sure to rinse out the brush in water and dry it with a paper towel in between colors. You may need several coats to achieve your desired shade. Let dry before hanging. (a)

2 For the gold lantern, evenly spray paint the lantern until it is covered. You may need several coats to achieve your desired shade. Let dry before hanging. (b)

3 Attach streamers, ribbons, and other desired ephemera to the lower metal parts of the painted lanterns. Bundle the three painted lanterns together and weave the craft wire in and out of the top metal portions of the lanterns to secure them together. Attach additional fold-out paper decorations to the bundle using craft wire. Trim excess wire with scissors.

a

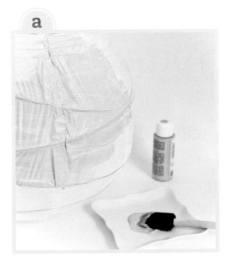

b

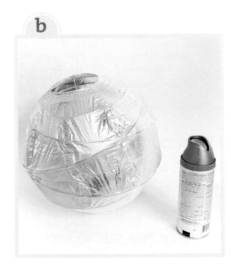

Three

Table
numbers

A piece of floral foam block, tucked into a votive candle holder, supports these elegant, understated table number displays. Heather used a dusty pink script font to create each number. Paired with small votives to fit the color scheme, these pennants add to the tablescapes in a beautifully functional way.

what you'll need*

Computer
Printer
White cardstock
Scissors
Wooden skewers
Gold spray paint
Floral foam block
Hot glue gun and glue stick
Small votives
Moss

Gather enough of these materials to make however many table numbers you need for your event.

what you do

1 Create the table numbers using a program on your computer (such as Word) and a desired font (elegant or casual, depending on the style of your wedding), spelling out each number. Print the numbers onto white cardstock, with enough white space between them to cut out the pennant shape. Also allow enough room on the left-hand straight edges to wrap around the wooden skewer. Each cutout pennant shown here measures approximately 1½ x 4 inches (3.8 x 10.2 cm). ⓐ

2 Insert wooden skewers into a floral foam block. Spray paint the skewers gold in a well-ventilated area. Let dry. ⓑ

3 Using a hot glue gun, attach each pennant to a wooden skewer by wrapping the straight edge around the skewer and gluing. ⓒ

4 Cut and insert pieces of the floral foam block to fit inside each votive candle holder. ⓓ

5 Top the pieces of foam with moss. Insert the table number pennants. ⓔⓕ

a

b

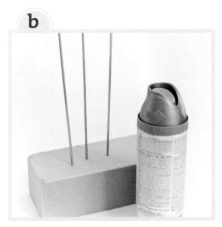

c

d

e

f

Vintage Wallpaper wrapping

With creamy pastel colors and unique patterns, vintage wallpaper makes great wrapping paper. You can wrap faux gifts as part of the décor, using them as a way to bring in more interest and color. When working with vintage wallpaper, use a hot glue gun to secure the edges—tape won't be strong enough for the heavy paper.

what you'll need

Vintage wallpaper
Empty boxes to wrap
Scissors
Hot glue gun and glue sticks
Assorted ribbons, millinery flowers,
   and charms

what you do

1 Cut a piece of wallpaper to fit
   the box to be wrapped. Fold
   down the edges of the paper and
   use a hot glue gun to seal the
   seam. ⓐ
2 Continue wrapping the box as
   you would a regular gift, but use
   the hot glue gun to adhere each
   seam where you would normally
   use tape. ⓑ ⓒ
3 Embellish with assorted
   vintage ribbons, millinery
   flowers, and charms.

Sources for Wallpaper

Your best bet for finding
vintage wallpaper is
through eBay. You can
find plenty of people
selling large rolls or
smaller sheets or even
a big lot of several rolls.
You can also find people
selling vintage wallpaper
through Etsy.

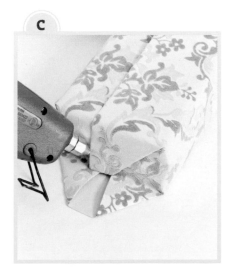

Photocopies for Wrapping Paper

Another way to incorporate
vintage images into your
wrapping is to photocopy
vintage greeting cards onto
printer paper. To make large
sheets similar to store-
bought wrapping paper,
take your greeting cards
to a local printer and make
large copies there. You can
then use the copied pages
to wrap gifts.

Wishing tree

Instead of a traditional guest book, Heather created this wishing tree for the happy couple. When guests sign their names on the back of the wish tags, they can also leave a wish or piece of advice. A fallen tree branch is the "tree" in this display. Urns come in all shapes and sizes, usually available at floral supply stores. Select one that is proportional to the branch size you want to use and the desired size of the finished tree.

what you'll need

Tree branch (proportionate in
   size to your urn)
Gold spray paint
Plaster of Paris
Small clay planter pot that fits
   inside urn
Plastic bag (optional)
Plastic wrap, 12 inches
   (30.5 cm) square
2 large rubber bands
Moss
Urn, approximately 12 inches
   (30.5 cm) tall or desired size
5 to 10 small silk flowers
Hot glue gun and glue sticks

what you do

1 Spray paint the tree branch
   gold in a well-ventilated
   area. ⓐ
2 Mix Plaster of Paris according
   to manufacturer's instruction
   and then pour into a small clay
   planter pot. (If the pot has a hole
   in the bottom, line it first with
   a plastic bag.) Quickly cover the
   pot with a piece of plastic wrap,
   and wrap rubber bands around
   the pot in opposite directions,
   as shown. ⓑ

3 While the plaster is still wet,
   insert the tree branch through
   the center opening of the
   rubber bands. Let dry. ⓒ
4 Fill the top of the plaster
   with moss. Place the pot in
   the urn. ⓓ
5 Use a hot glue gun to attach silk
   flowers to some of the twigs of
   the branch. ⓔ
6 Tie several Wishing Tree Tags
   (see page 96) onto the branches.

a

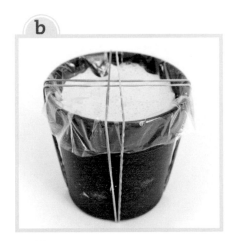
b

c

d

e

Wishing Tree tags

To create wishing tree tags, Heather used copies of vintage photos. Including old photos of family members' weddings would be a lovely nod to heritage. You could also use engagement photos of the bride and groom instead of vintage ones. Standard circular reinforcement tabs can be found in office supply stores. However, if you're lucky, you might find vintage ones either online or at a thrift store.

what you'll need

Vintage photos

White cardstock

Pinking shears

¼-inch (6 mm) hole punch

Reinforcement tabs: vintage or new

Glue stick

what you do

1 Photocopy old photos onto white cardstock. (a)

2 Cut each photo out with pinking shears. (b)

3 Punch a hole in the top of each card. (c)

4 Adhere reinforcement tabs over the holes with a glue stick. (d)

5 Thread and secure a piece of twine through the reinforcement tabs for each card.

a

b

c

d

Wishing Tag Instructions

So your guests know what to do with the wishing tags, consider making a small sign to instruct them. A simple handwritten sign backed with cardstock and taped to a vintage photo holder will help them know what to write.

French-Inspired wedding

with Corey Amaro

www.willows95988.typepad.com

For the bride who's looking to be authentic royalty for a day, here's a French-inspired wedding sure to catch your eye. As an American artist living in France, Corey Amaro is intensely familiar with the tradition and style of Old World France—and she's had years of experience as a French antique dealer, buying antique French textiles and ephemera for international clients, for their shops and personal collections. If your heart lies in the royal traditions, grand tapestries, and fancy brocades of old Provence, take a page from Corey's book to inspire your special day.

antique paper and textiles

Opulent, antique textiles and centuries-old paper goods are the foundation for this French-inspired wedding. After all, what could be more romantic than aged love letters written in French, and antique millinery flowers so beautiful they could have been seen on a hat worn by a courted young lady? If you don't have a broad collection of French antiques, don't worry—the more you look the luckier you will be. Start with local antique shops, but also look online. People often seek to rid their homes of what may be "junk" to them, but may be the perfect piece of decorative paper or textile to you. Of course reproductions would also work well.

Even if you find just a bit of decorative paper, make photocopies of whatever you find, and reuse it over and over. Copied on beige paper, old pages from books will look aged, and since many of the papers will be used in décor, guests won't notice the repeated patterns. Many companies are making beautiful scrapbook paper and fabrics as well, so don't be discouraged if you're not able to use authentic antique materials in all your projects. Any beautiful paper or fabric with that timeworn feel will work.

old world culture and customs

The French culture is rich with classic recipes and customs that will only enhance the theme at your wedding. Corey made the classic French wedding cake, pièce montée, for this celebration, stacking cream puffs in a pyramid, and filling in the gaps with fresh whipped cream. She also brought in traditional religious symbols, such as the banner and even the ribbon used in the invitations, for a hint of antique France. With luxurious decorative elements, delicious food, and a peek at antique Provence at every turn, guests at this wedding will feel like they stepped into another century, one rich with ribbons, royalty, and romance.

Corey's Advice for Newlyweds
Kiss each other before leaving the house each day, and again before going to bed at night.

Corey's Simple Ways to Cut Costs

- If you don't have enough decorative paper in your collection, make photocopies instead of buying more.
- Use scraps of fabric whenever possible—in the boutonnieres, wedding headband, and garter.

Bridal
veil

Corey aimed to use all antique French textiles in her projects, and this veil is no exception—a scrap of tulle for the headband, millinery flowers, and a large piece of tulle for the veil piece all came from her fabric collection. Take a look at your own fabric collection to see what you could use for this veil, or ask your family, friends, and the local antique store dealer to keep their eyes open for structurally sound, yet pretty, textiles. This project is made up of three different sections, but all three pieces can stand on their own.

what you'll need

2 yards (1.8 m) of ivory tulle,
   2½ inches (6.4 cm) wide
280 tulle fabric rosettes,
   ¼ inch (6 mm) in diameter
60 tulle fabric rosettes,
   ½ inch (1.3 cm) in diameter
Hand-sewing needle
Gold-colored thread
Scissors
Bobby pins
Antique millinery flowers
5 yards (4.6 m) of ivory tulle (or as
   long as you want the veil piece to
   be), 2 yards (1.8 m) wide

what you do

1 **Headband and garland:**
   • Lay the 2-yard (1.8 m) piece of narrow tulle on a flat surface.
   • Sew the rosettes in three rows down the length of it, using a hand-sewing needle and gold thread. Place the larger rosettes in the middle and the smaller rosettes on the outside rows, making sure that all rosettes are touching. ⓐ ⓑ
   • Bobby pin the tulle as a headband across the bride's forehead, weaving the excess ends down through her hair.

2 **Millinery flowers:** Bobby pin the antique millinery flowers directly into the bride's hair. ⓒ

3 **The veil:** Bobby pin the 5-yard (4.6 m) piece of tulle to the back of the bride's head, and also to the garland woven through her hair. Let the veil fall naturally down her back.

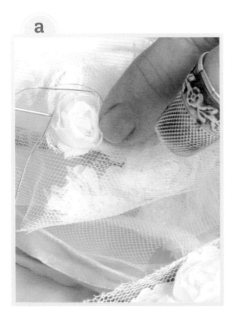

a

b

c

cornet de
Confetti

In France, a famous wedding tradition involves throwing small tissue-paper hearts on the bride and groom as they exit the ceremony. This confetti holder is inspired by this act, but it is filled with rose petals instead of paper hearts. You could also fill the container with small treats for children. This project is perfect for repurposing antique paper goods and scraps. If you have antique pieces of paper you don't want to use, make copies of them on beige paper and use the copied paper in these projects.

what you'll need

2 sheets of decorative paper, each
   8½ x 11 inches (21.6 x 27.9 cm)

Scissors

Glue stick

Antique gold wire French fringe

Small paper cup

Black marker

Mini clothespin

Millinery flower

Dried rose petals

what you do

1 Cut one sheet of decorative
   paper into a 6 x 11-inch
   (15.2 x 27.9 cm) rectangle.
   Starting at one of the short ends,
   roll up the paper to make a cone.
   Leave a small opening at the
   pointed end. Glue into place. ⓐ

2 Cut a short piece of gold
   fringe. Roll it up, apply glue
   to the bound edge, and insert
   that end into the bottom of
   the cornet. ⓑ ⓒ

3 Cut a second sheet of decorative
   paper into 6 circles, using a
   small paper cup or round lid as
   a circle template. ⓓ

4 Glue a millinery flower to a
   clothespin. ⓔ

5 Use the decorative clothespin
   to pin the decorative circle to
   the front of the cornet. Fill the
   cornet with dried rose petals.

a

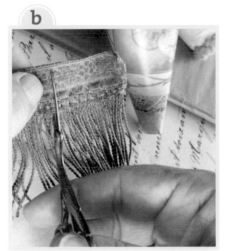

b

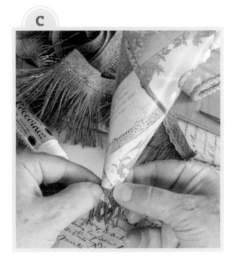

c

d

e

Good Advice

If you like, encourage guests
to use the circle cutouts (in
step 3) as a place to write
down a bit of advice for the
bride and groom. Instead of
plain decorative paper, write
"My Advice for the Bride and
Groom" on one of the circles,
make copies, and cut them
out to attach to the cornet.

Ring Bearer's Case

A jewelry case seems the most logical place to house rings, so why not use it as the official vessel for the ring bearer? You can also dress up the jewelry box by filling it with dried roses on which to rest the rings.

Crystal
dinner
menu

Corey knew she wanted to use large French crystals for this project, so when she came upon antique church crystals, she was overjoyed. They were beautiful, in a stunning shape, and big enough that the menu card fit in the outline of them. Corey used antique marriage documents to create this menu, but any antique-looking decorative paper will do.

what you'll need

Crystals that are flat on one side, approximately 3 x 7 inches (7.6 x 17.8 cm)

Pencil

2 sheets of decorative paper

Sharp craft scissors

Glue stick

Black fine-point permanent marker

10 inches (25.4 cm) of silk ribbon, ⅜ inch (9.5 mm) wide

Millinery velvet flower

what you do

1. Lay the crystal on a sheet of decorative paper and trace it lightly. Cut it out and glue it, right side up, to the back of the crystal. This will be the side you will see on the front of the crystal. ⓐ

2. Fold a second sheet of decorative paper in half. Lay the crystal down, aligning one side with the folded edge, and trace again.

3. Cut out the crystal shape without cutting on the folded edge. Open this folded paper like a card and write the dinner menu on the inside. ⓑ

4. Glue the front of the folded paper to the paper glued to the back of the crystal.

5. Push the silk ribbon through the hole at the top of the crystal and tie. Glue the velvet millinery flower to the top of the crystal.

a

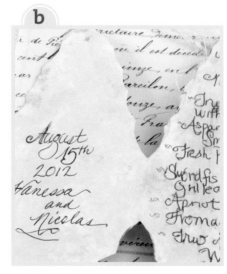

b

Stunning Place Settings

For a fancy dinner to remember, stack the bread plate and salad plate on top of the dinner plate. Then place a folded cloth napkin, a thick piece of satin ribbon, and the crystal dinner menu on top of the plates. Crystal goblets and fine silverware complete the tablescape.

Wedding invitation

In France, wedding invitations come in large envelopes, so that even before the recipients open them, they know what to expect inside. The quality of the materials used is a testament to the importance of the event. To add to the special nature of such an item, Corey added wide ribbons to her invitation, a nod to the French tradition of governing officials and high members of society wearing wide ribbon sashes for major holidays and events. The tools and materials listed below are what you'll need for each invitation, so make sure to adjust the quantity depending on your guest list. All products can be bought new, or search your local antique stores for pretty papers to use.

what you'll need

5-inch-wide (12.7 cm) cream envelope

Scissors

Decorative music paper or sheet music

Glue stick

8½-inch-wide (21.6 cm) cream envelope

2 pieces of antique French cardstock (or other cardstock): 4 x 7½ inches (10.2 x 19 cm)

Pencil

Black permanent marker

Antique cardstock with scalloped edges (or other decorative cardstock) trimmed to fit the smaller cream envelope

Letters, cut out of paper (or circle-punched and rubber-stamped cardstock): U, I, 2 N's, and 2 O's

24-inch (61 cm) piece of antique cream moiré ribbon, 6 inches (15.2 cm) wide with fringe edges*, cut as follows (the measurement includes the fringe):

- 1 piece that is 8 inches (20.3 cm) with fringe edge
- 1 piece that is 16 inches (40.6 cm) with fringe edge

Sewing machine

2 pieces of decorative fringe edging (unless your wide ribbon already has fringe edges), each 6 inches (15.2 cm)

8 inches (20.3 cm) of champagne silk ribbon, 1½ inches (3.8 cm) wide

Antique champagne silk flower

If your moiré ribbon doesn't have a fringed edge, find a fringe you like and sew it to one short edge of each ribbon.

what you do

1 Cut out a piece of decorative paper to partially line the interior of the smaller cream envelope, including the triangle flap. Glue in place using a glue stick. Repeat for the larger cream envelope. ⓐ

2 With a pencil, lightly draw a rounded decorative M shape on the bottom of the cardstock. Cut out the shape and discard the pieces. Continuing with the pencil, draw decoratively around the entire edge of the cardstock and write out the wedding invitation. Go back over the words with a black permanent marker. ⓑ

3 On the second piece of cardstock, trace a decorative edge with the pencil and write the event details including wedding registry, directions to the event, and so forth.

4 Write the RSVP note on the antique French card with scalloped edges, and insert it into the small envelope along with the cutout children's letters for a "oui" or a "non" reply.

5 Fold the 16-inch piece of ribbon in half, and insert the 8-inch (20.3 cm) piece into the fold. Insert the wedding announcement card in between the front ribbon and the middle ribbon, and the wedding detail page in between the middle ribbon and the back ribbon. ⓒ

6 Stitch across the top of the ribbon pieces and cards, where the fold is, to secure.

7 Tie a small knot in each end of the 8-inch (20.3 cm) piece of champagne silk ribbon, and sew across the top seam of the book.

8 To finish, sew on the silk flower and tuck the RSVP card behind the wedding detail page.

a

b

c

Wedding Cake Topper

For a truly French-inspired wedding, create a pièce montée—cream puffs stacked in a pyramid for your guests to enjoy. This classic wedding cake pairs well with a small crown topper that honors France's royalty throughout the centuries, most notably King Louis the Sixteenth and Marie Antoinette (fitting for cake!).

Fleur-de-Lys Backdrop Banner

Banners symbolize royalty, and marriages are certainly royal in significance. An antique banner similar to this one would have been carried in religious ceremonies several centuries ago. Use an existing curtain panel or sew up a panel with cream and light-blue fabrics. Cut fleur-de-lys shapes out of gold tissue paper and adhere them the fabric panel with a glue stick. Place it as a decorative item, behind the cake as a backdrop.

Rustic and Elegant
diy wedding

with tracy schultz

www.re-purposely.com

If your idea of a party is an elegant picnic held in the great outdoors, look no further than this one-of-a-kind event put together by Tracy Schultz for the wedding of her daughter, Erin. The natural environment and handpicked wildflowers lent an organic, beautiful feel to the day, while intimate wedding projects added elegance and personality.

a festive reflection of the couple

Erin and Parker's wedding took place on a ranch in Orange County, California. The rustic terrain mixed with elegant elements to create an overall feeling of a picnic that could have taken place in the 1920s. Upon arrival, guests were greeted by charming hand-painted wood signs, directing them to the ceremony and reception site, where they were met with displays of vintage suitcases, old family photos, and chalkboard-painted accessories atop antique desks and tables. Artful arrangements of wildflowers, white linens, photos of the couple, and creatively repurposed projects covered each corner of the gathering space.

Burlap and baby's breath set the stage for the elegant dinner party, while simple white candles and twinkle lights provided ambiance. Erin glowed in a vintage wedding dress and headpiece with finger curls in her hair to add to the festive nature of the event.

Tracy's Simple Ways to Cut Costs

- Learn the ins and outs of your local thrift stores for good deals and finds.
- Repurpose, repurpose, repurpose! Even the simplest of items can be transformed.

Tracy's Advice for Newlyweds

Pray together on a daily basis, forgive each other always, and seek out the best in each other—you'll usually find what you're looking for!

simple and organic
with a vintage twist

The DIY elements that Tracy created set the stage to highlight this very special day. The guest book, doily lamps, table settings, signs, and chandeliers were all purposefully designed to be simple and organic with a vintage twist. Tracy relied on items from her family's collection to be the base of many of the projects—even going so far as to repurpose an old-fashioned alarm clock as the cake topper!

Handmade invitations and thank-you cards designed with twine, kraft paper, and hints of lace married perfectly with the classic burlap, clean white linens,

and fresh flowers covering the dinner tables, making the theme cohesive and elegant.

The wedding party gathered flowers to fill the handmade planter boxes the morning of the wedding, while family members came together to bring in furniture and arrange tables and décor. Tracy and Erin's intensive search for chandeliers paid off when the beautiful fixtures were hung from the trees as if in a fairytale. With love, hard work, and a dash of time, Tracy created a romantic, elegant haven in the great outdoors—a true party that no one wanted to leave.

Handmade
wedding invitations

Tracy wanted a natural and organic feel for the invitations. She didn't want them to look overly feminine, but instead look handmade. And she wanted to use recycled materials where possible. She ordered an address stamp (see Resources, page 143), which saved her from having to write out the return address hundreds of times.

what you'll need

Natural muslin fabric: 4 x 6 inches (10.2 x 15.2 cm) (torn and ironed)*

Custom invitation stamp and initial stamp (see Resources, page 143)

Extra-large black inkpad (see Resources, page 143)

Temporary spray adhesive

White cardstock: 4½ x 6½ inches (11.4 x 16.5 cm)**

Sewing machine with heavy-duty sewing machine needle

Computer with Adobe Illustrator and Microsoft Word

Local or home printer

Printer paper

Three-tab file folders, made from natural brown recycled paper

Scissors

Pencil or kitchen knife

¼-inch (6 mm) hole punch

Doily rubber stamp

White inkpad

8-inch (20.3 cm) round paper doilies*

Hemp yarn: 74 inches (188 cm)*

Invitation envelopes, size A7*

*one per invitation
** two per invitation

what you do

1 Make the invitation.
   - On a hard surface, stamp the invitation stamp onto the muslin using an extra-large black inkpad. Spray temporary spray adhesive to the back of the muslin piece and center it onto the cardstock piece. (a)
   - Sew the muslin to the cardstock using a sewing machine and a heavy-duty needle, leaving a ¼-inch (6 mm) border. (b)

2 Create a map to the wedding using Adobe Illustrator on your computer. Use Word to create your Details card. Send both files to a local printer or print on your own computer.

3 Create your Reply card in Word, making sure that each card measures 4½ x 6½ inches (11.4 x 16.5 cm). Send the file to a local printer or print on your own computer using white cardstock. Stamp the Initial stamp on the back side of the card. (c)

4 Make the brown envelope.
   - With the file folder closed, cut it to 5¼ x 10¼ inches (13.3 x 26 cm), with the existing centerfold on one long side; it will become the centerfold on the invitation folder. (Save the scrap pieces of the file folder to use in the Thank You cards.)
   - Open the cut folder and fold it up from the bottom 4¾ inches (12 cm) to make the pocket for the inserts. Press on the fold with the side of a pencil or the dull side of a kitchen knife to flatten the crease.
   - With the folder open, punch holes approximately at the midpoint, through both layers and on both sides of the folder.
   - Stamp the Doily stamp with the white inkpad on the front of the folder. Let dry.
   - Stamp the Initial stamp with the blank inkpad over the Doily stamp imprint. (d)

5 Assemble the invitation.
   - Cut off the bottom portion of a paper doily; fold it in half, and place in folder. (e)
   - Insert all cards into the folder. Insert hemp yarn though the holes, and wrap it around the invitation folder several times before tying it into a bow. (f)
   - Use an A7 envelope for mailing; extra postage will be required.

a

b

c

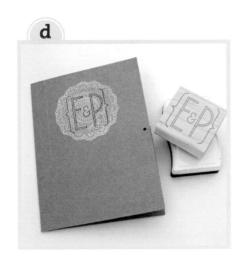

d

e

f

Thank You Notes

Use the leftover scrap pieces of file folders from your wedding invitations as the front of your Thank You cards. Stamp the Doily stamp and Initial stamp on the front, then cut a piece of white cardstock to fit on the back where you will write your note. The cards should fit in a No. 4 envelope to mail.

Advice Tags
and clothespins

These advice tags and clothespins were used with the Marriage Advice Chalkboard Mailbox (page 117) at the wedding, where guests wrote out their marriage advice and well wishes for the couple and placed it in the mailbox. Later, the tags were added to a keepsake book for the bride and groom that included these tags as well as recipes collected from family and friends at Erin's wedding showers.

what you'll need

Strong coffee

Paper plate

Shipping tags with reinforced holes,
   4¾ x 2⅜ inch (12 x 6 cm)

Paper grocery bag

Coffee cup or Mason jar

¼-inch (6 mm) vintage lace: 2⅜ inch
   (6 cm) piece for each tag

Sewing machine

Wooden clothespins

Assorted paper ephemera such
   as pages from a book and
   sheet music

Mod Podge

Sandpaper

what you do

1 Make some strong coffee and set it aside to cool—your fingers will be much obliged! Remove the string from the tags. Pour a small amount of the coffee onto a sturdy paper plate. Dip the tags into the coffee, then shake off the excess coffee and place the tag on a paper grocery bag to dry.

2 When the tags are dry, dip a coffee cup or mason jar into the coffee and set it onto the tags in various places to leave a ring on the tags. Let dry. ⓐ

3 Sew vintage lace to the bottom of each tag with a sewing machine. ⓑ

4 Cut strips of paper ephemera to fit your clothespins. Use Mod Podge to glue the paper to the clothespins and let dry. ⓒ

5 Lightly sand and repeat with another coat of Mod Podge. Let dry.

Coffee Dyeing Tips

You can dye your tags in coffee anywhere, but if you're in a hurry, do it outside on a warm day—the tags will be dry before you know it. Also, it is best to let your tags dry on thick paper, such as a brown paper grocery bag, in order for the excess to be absorbed by the bag. The coffee tends to pool on a plastic bag, so the drying process will be longer.

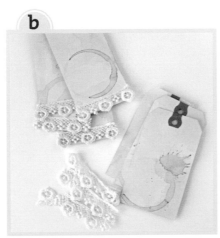

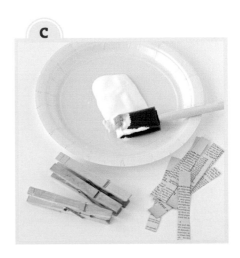

Mr. and Mrs. *Forks*

Tracy collected china and silver for all of the 200+ place settings for this wedding. She began searching more than six months in advance for the event, scouring flea markets and thrift stores the world over. This silver-stamping project was a natural progression for making the bride and groom's place settings a bit more personal. Once she got the stamping, Tracy quickly realized that she needed a bit more strength to get a good, clean imprint, so she enlisted her husband's help.

what you'll need

2 silver-plated forks
Silver polish (optional)
Steel ⅛-inch (3 mm) letter/number
   stamping kit (available at your
   local hardware store)
Mallet
Black acrylic paint
Dry rag

what you do

1 Polish forks with silver polish, if necessary.
2 Using letter stamps and the mallet, stamp "MR" on one fork and "MRS" on the other. ⓐ
3 Rub a dab of black acrylic paint over the stamped letters, and wipe off excess paint with a dry rag. ⓑ

Bride and Groom Mason Jar Goblets

Tracy used pint-sized mason jars and striped paper straws for all the guests' drinks, so she decided to elevate the bride and groom's glasses a bit with candlestick bases. To make these, she used stronghold glue to adhere the bottom of the jar to the top of the candlestick and then let them dry. They were adorable next to the vintage china, silver, and muslin knotted napkins.

Vintage Doily
table runner

For the tablecloths, Tracy purchased a large roll of canvas, and the day of the wedding, she rolled them out on the long tables, tore the ends, and left them frayed. A length of burlap ran down the center of the tables over the canvas. For the bride and groom's table, she added this simple and elegant vintage doily table runner to bring the whole look together.

what you'll need

Doilies of all shapes and sizes: approximately
   20 to cover an 8-foot (2.4 m) table
Hand-sewing needle
White perle cotton
Scissors

what you do

1 Plan out your arrangement of doilies by
   laying the biggest doilies on the floor in
   a serpentine line with spaces in between
   them. Fill in the spaces with the smaller
   doilies, overlapping the edges. Be sure
   to alternate the doily sizes so you get an
   interesting shape. (a)

2 Using a needle and white perle cotton,
   sew the doilies together by double
   knotting at various places to keep them
   securely in place. (b)

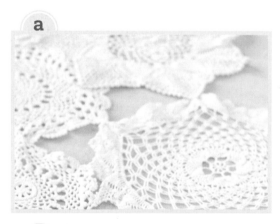

Chalk It Up

Chalkboard paint instantly personalizes and charms any piece of décor. Tracy used it to cover a globe, as well as several pieces of glass and Masonite to fit inside picture frames. She also applied chalkboard paint to a vintage mailbox to hold the Advice Tags and Clothespins (page 126). A few cute messages later, and they were an instant success.

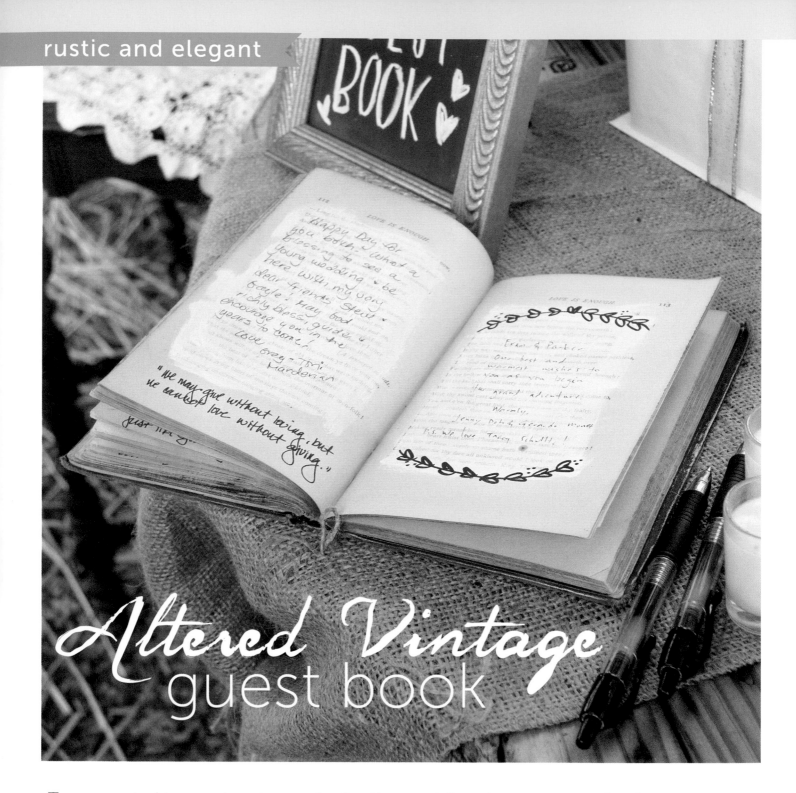

Altered Vintage guest book

Tracy wanted to create a keepsake for the wedding that was completely repurposed and unique—plus, she wanted it to be small enough that the bride and groom could keep it in their small Brooklyn apartment. Guests wrote well wishes for the happy couple on the altered pages.

what you'll need

Vintage book
White glue
3 metal clamps
Sharp craft knife
Gold acrylic paint
2 foam brushes
White gesso
Black permanent markers (thick and
  thin widths)
Family photos
Photo mount corners

what you do

1 Create an inset for a photograph of the bride and groom: (a)
   • Glue enough pages together to form the inset. Use clamps to hold the book in place and let dry completely. (b)
   • Carefully cut out the inset box using a sharp craft knife. Paint the inset portion of the pages with gold paint, as well as a thin line around the cutout portion to make a frame. (c)
2 Paint pages throughout the book with a thin coat of gesso, leaving a border of print around the page. You should be able to read the written words from the book through the gesso. Let dry. Creatively outline the gessoed pages with a permanent marker. (d)
3 Add the love story of the bride and groom to the front of the book with permanent markers. (e)
4 Mount wedding photos of parents and grandparents on some of the pages of the book using the photo mount corners. You could even place a "Reserved" tag on the page to the right of the photo in order for the appropriate person(s) to be able to sign next to their photo. (f)

Iron Gate Chandelier

Tracy wanted a simple and rustic chandelier to accompany the more formal and elegant crystal chandelier that she purchased at the Antique Rose Bowl Flea Market in Pasadena, California. Her solution was to combine an old iron gate, wire, mason jars, and candles for the perfect juxtaposition.

Vintage Doily
balloon lamps

If you like the look of a vintage doily light, but would prefer not to have to pull out the sewing needle, this is your solution. Tracy used a simple paste to adhere the doilies to a blown-up balloon. Once the doilies were dried, she popped the balloon and inserted a light kit. This project does take several days to complete—Tracy covered about half of each balloon at a time, then waited a day to cover the rest of it, and then let the doilies dry on the balloon for at least three days. Patience will reward your efforts, with a stunning display of light and shadows.

what you'll need

Plastic drop cloth

Homemade paste (see recipe on
    opposite page)

32-inch (81.3 cm) balloons

Hand pump for the balloons

5-gallon bucket for each
    balloon lamp

Cheap 2-inch (5.1 cm) wide
    painting brush

Disposable rubber gloves

Vintage doilies in various shapes and
    sizes (approximately 10 to 12 for
    one lamp)

Hand-sewing needle

Embroidery floss

Cream or white spray paint (optional)

Spray varnish sealant: matte or
    satin finish

Hard plastic scrap for the light
    template, like a clean, empty
    gallon milk container

Light kit

what you do

1 Cover your working area with a plastic drop cloth. Make a batch of homemade paste. Following Tracy's lead, you will be coating one-half a balloon at a time, so one batch of paste is enough for now.

2 Using the hand pump, blow up the balloon to your desired size, knot it, and place it on a 5-gallon bucket with the knot facing downward. Since you'll be working over a few days to cover the balloon, this will allow you to finish with the knot facing upward in the correct position.

3 Lightly coat half of the balloon with the glue mixture and a paintbrush. Wearing your disposable gloves, dip 5 to 6 doilies at a time in the glue mixture, wring them out and set them aside.

4 Start layering the doilies onto the balloon, making sure to overlap them at least 1 inch (2.5 cm) on all edges for added strength. Use the paintbrush to cover both the balloon base and the doily with the glue. Continue until about half of the balloon is covered. Cover the doilies on the balloon with a final thin layer of glue and let them dry on the bucket for about 12 hours. ⓐ

5 Make a new batch of homemade paste. Turn the balloon over and finish covering the balloon. Leave an area at the center top of the balloon (around the knot) empty so there is a hole large enough for your light to pass through, approximately 2½ inches (6.4 cm) in diameter. Be sure to cover the dried portion of the balloon with the fresh paste before layering with the new doilies. Once the balloon is covered with doilies, coat them with a final layer of glue. Let the

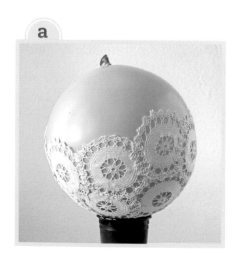

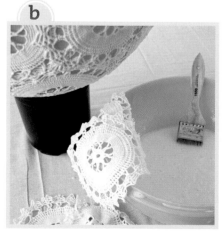

balloon completely dry; it may take up to three days, depending on temperature and weather conditions. ⓑ

6 When the Doily Lamp is completely dry, you should be able to pull the balloon away from the doilies by inserting your hand through the top hole (that was left for the light kit), running it around the balloon, and gently separating it from the doilies as you go along. While holding onto the balloon knot, pop the balloon with a needle and try to release the air slowly.

7 You may need to add a few stitches with embroidery floss to better secure errant doilies in place. The Doily Lamp should be hard to the touch.

8 If your doilies have discolored during the glue process, you may want to spray them with a coat or two of spray paint. Let it dry if you do so. Then, spray the entire balloon with 2 to 3 coats of a matte spray varnish/sealer for added strength. Let dry.

9 To make a reinforcement to hold the light kit in place, trace the circle opening of the light fixture onto a piece of scrap plastic and cut out the center of the circle. Then trace a rectangle around the center circle, and cut out the rectangle. Your rectangle should be approximately 6 x 3 inches (15.2 x 7.6 cm).

10 Screw the light fixture without the light bulb onto the piece of plastic, then screw in the light bulb. ⓒ

11 Bending the plastic, squeeze the light fixture into the balloon opening. Pull up on the cord and the plastic should lock in place.

Homemade Paste Recipe

½ cup flour
4 cups water
3 tablespoons sugar
½ cup Elmer's glue

1 In a large mixing bowl, mix the flour and 2 cups of the water and set aside.

2 In a large saucepan, bring the remaining 2 cups water to a boil; add the flour mixture and return to a boil. Remove from heat.

3 Add the sugar and Elmer's glue. Let cool; it will thicken.

This recipe makes enough paste for half of a 32-inch (81.3 cm) balloon.

About the Contributors

in order of appearance

Serena Thompson lives in the countryside of eastern Washington State with her husband and four sons. A passionate entrepreneur, Serena is the founder of The Farm Chicks Antiques Show. In addition, she has authored two books and works as a magazine editor. As a stay-at-home-mom with a knack for thrifty creativity, she strives daily to make a happy home for her family. To learn more about Serena, visit *www.thefarmchicks.com*.

Minna Mercke Schmidt lives in southern Sweden, where she works as a creative photographer. Six years ago, Minna created Blomsterverkstad, a company that produces lifestyle articles, publishes books, and helps other companies find their style in marketing. With a passion for flowers, DIY, and finding beauty in everyday life, she shares many of her current projects on her personal blog. To learn more about Minna, visit *www.blomsterverkstad.com*.

Tiffany Kirchner-Dixon is a self-proclaimed romantic, dreamer, and fancy farm girl. She lives with her husband and two daughters on a farm just outside Seattle, Washington. A professional photographer by day and an artist and rodeo cowgirl by night, Tiffany infuses a bit of her personal style into everything she does. To learn more about Tiffany, visit *www.thefancyfarmgirl.com* and *www.thefancyfarmgirlphotography.com*.

Heather Bullard is a stylist, photographer, and editorial story producer, residing in Southern California with her husband and daughter. Her fresh approach to vintage style has led to her current roles as Contributing Editor for *Country Living Magazine* and Editor-in-Chief for *Souvenir Magazine*. Heather embraces creativity daily while scouting locations, styling sets, and posting to her popular lifestyle blog. To learn more about Heather, visit *www.heatherbullard.com*.

About the Contributors
continued

Tracy Schultz is an artistic jack-of-all-trades who lives in Southern California alongside her husband of nearly 30 years, a spoiled Chihuahua, and a feisty cat. Always eager to share her creative passion with other artists, Tracy enjoys attending and teaching classes at Studio CRESCENDOh in Santa Ana, California. She recently opened an Etsy shop where she sells vintage finds and recycled treasures. To learn more about Tracy, visit www.*re-purposely.com*.

Corey Amaro is a California native living in France with her husband, a Frenchman she married 25 years ago. While living abroad, Corey has turned her passion for French flea markets into a successful business, selling her antique treasures across the globe. She shares stories, photos, and all of her best vintage finds on her daily blog. To learn more about Corey, visit www.*willows95988.typepad.com*.

Resources

Corey Amaro

Hairstylist: Manuella Carletti
Marseille/Aix en Provence
hairmoving@hotmail.fr
(011 33) 06 17 79 82 49

Tongue in Cheek Antiques
Marseille and Aix en Provence
coreyamaro@aol.com
www.willows95988.typepad.com

Heather Bullard

Flower & Water
Lindsay LeMone
www.FlowerAndWater.com

Co-styling: Pam Garrison
www.pamgarrison.typepad.com

Head shot: Nick Francis

Tiffany Kirchner-Dixon

Jewelry worn by models courtesy of
Beth Quinn Designs
www.bethquinndesigns.com

Hollywood lighted frame co-created
by Cindy Dockins
www.tarte.us

Head shot: Kayla Carlin

Minna Merke Schmidt
Head shot: Robert Schmidt

Tracy Schultz
Hugh Forte Photography
www.hughforte.com

Cynthia Shaffer Photography
www.cynthiashaffer.com

Parker Young Photography
www.parkeryoung.net

Eric Hires 16mm Weddings
www.erichires.com

Flowers: Morgan Schultz

Lettering: Christa Schultz

Food: Orange County Catering
www.orangecountycatering.com

Rentals: Atlas Rentals
www.atlasparty.com

Music: Anthony Batista
New York, NY

Serena Thompson
Concept collaboration and co-
styling: Alisa Lewis Event Design
www.alisaevents.com

Furniture and wedding materials,
supplies: The Attic | A Vintage
Rental Company
www.atticrentals.com

Ifong Chen Photographer
www.ifongphotography.com

Venue: Cable Creek Farm
www.cablecreekfarm.com

Flowers: Fleurtations Floral
www.fleurtationsfloral.com

Bride's Dress: Carousel
www.facebook.com/carouseljenny

Veil: Stella's Design
www.stellasdesign.com

Food: Feast Catering Company
www.feastcateringco.com

Crepe Cake: Erin Blackburn

Truck for band stage:
Murren Family

Music: Rockin' B Ranch
Bluegrass Band
www.rockinbranch.com

Hair: Camille Cuts Me
www.facebook.com/camillecutsme

Make-up: Shasta Hankins
www.shastahankins.com

Dishes, Glassware, and Silverware:
Event Rents
www.event-rents.com

Herbs & Tea: Sweet Roots
www.sweetroots.blogspot.com

Herbs: Hansen's Farm
www.hansensgreenblufforchard.com

Herbs: Strawberry Hill Farm
(509) 238-6919

Special thanks to the bridal party:
Bride and Groom: Rose and
Pete Cowger
Bridesmaids: Kaitlin Ellithorpe,
Amy Ellithorpe, and
Elizabeth Stadley
Groomsmen: Alex Murren, Aaron
Adkinson, and Jake Stadley

Editor: **LINDA KOPP**
Art Director: **KRISTI PFEFFER**
Graphic Designer: **RAQUEL JOYA**
Cover Designer: **KRISTI PFEFFER**
Writer: **AMANDA CRABTREE WESTON**
Copyeditor: **NANCY D. WOOD**
Assistant Editors: **KERRI WINTERSTEIN, MONICA MOUET**

Index

About the Author

Jenny Doh is head of *www.crescendoh.com*. She has authored and packaged numerous books including *Craft-a-Doodle*, *Crochet Love*, *Print Collective*, *Creative Lettering*, *Stamp It!*, *Journal It!*, *We Make Dolls!*, *Hand in Hand*, and *Signature Styles*. She lives in Santa Ana, California, and loves to create, stay fit, and play music.